LIFE IN COLONIAL AMERICA

by Julia Garstecki

Content Consultant
Louise Breen
Associate Professor of History
Kansas State University

Core Library

An Imprint of Abdo Publishing
www.abdopublishing.com

www.abdopublishing.com

Published by Abdo Publishing, a division of ABDO, PO Box 398166,
Minneapolis, Minnesota 55439. Copyright © 2015 by Abdo Consulting
Group, Inc. International copyrights reserved in all countries. No part of
this book may be reproduced in any form without written permission from
the publisher. Core Library™ is a trademark and logo of Abdo Publishing.

Printed in the United States of America, North Mankato, Minnesota
092014
012015

THIS BOOK CONTAINS
RECYCLED MATERIALS

Cover Photo: North Wind Picture Archives/AP Images
Interior Photos: North Wind Picture Archives, 4, 8, 10, 12, 15, 17, 18, 21,
23, 26, 29, 31, 33, 34, 36, 40, 42, 45; Red Line Editorial, 28, 39

Editor: Ethan Hiedeman
Series Designer: Becky Daum

Library of Congress Control Number: 2014944195

Cataloging-in-Publication Data
Garstecki, Julia.
 Life in Colonial America / Julia Garstecki.
   p. cm. -- (Daily life in US history)
ISBN 978-1-62403-630-9 (lib. bdg.)
Includes bibliographical references and index.
1. United States--Social life and customs--To 1775--Juvenile literature.   I.
Title.
973--dc23
                                                        2014944195

CONTENTS

CHAPTER ONE

EUROPEANS COME TO AMERICA

In 1492 Italian explorer Christopher Columbus thought he had discovered a new world. He had sailed from Spain across the Atlantic Ocean. He had spent the last five weeks at sea. His crew grew restless, afraid that they would never make landfall and return home again. But then the crew started to see birds flying and vegetation floating in the water. These were signs that land was nearby. Columbus's

Columbus's first voyage across the Atlantic consisted of three ships: the *Niña*, the *Pinta*, and the *Santa María*.

Mystery at Roanoke

The first would-be English colonists landed on the coast of North Carolina in 1584. The English tried to settle on Roanoke Island. But tensions with the local Native Americans and lack of supplies forced the settlers to leave. The English tried to settle Roanoke again in 1587. The second expedition to Roanoke Island met with a mysterious end. When a ship bringing provisions returned to the colony in 1590, the settlement was deserted. Some historians think hostile Native Americans wiped out the group. Others think the group left to live among the Native Americans. But to this day no one knows for sure what happened to the Lost Colony.

ships sighted land on October 12. Columbus had hoped to find a faster route to India and China. He didn't find it. Instead he landed in modern-day Haiti in the Caribbean Sea.

The world he found was new only to Europeans. Native peoples had inhabited the land for centuries. They had their own beliefs and customs that were unfamiliar to the Europeans. These differences—and the European desire for land—would eventually lead to conflicts and in some cases war.

Columbus's arrival in 1492 laid the groundwork for the period known as Colonial America. It was a time of great change. European powers including England, Spain, and France established colonies in what would one day become the United States of America. European colonists pushed many Native Americans off their land. More Native Americans died from violence and disease. Settlers continued to pour across the Atlantic.

Crossing the Atlantic

The trip across the Atlantic Ocean took between one and six months, depending on weather and the sailing experience of the crew. Ships sometimes traveled just five miles (8 km) in a day. There were no private cabins for the colonists. They slept on the floor. Dinner was salted beef and a dry biscuit, and those might be infested with bugs. Drinking water got contaminated. It was too dangerous to have a fire on the ship for

Would-be colonists brought with them only what they could carry and fit into their allotted space on the ships that would take them to the New World.

heat, so colonists endured cold nights. Illness was common and killed many passengers.

Opportunity

Many people came to the New World for a better life. Others came because they had no choice. Europe's economies were struggling. Finding work was difficult, and people were unable to buy land in Europe. English trading companies, such as the Virginia Company, found a solution. They offered employment and land to those willing to develop new colonies in different parts of the world.

Religious Freedom

Some Europeans sailed to the New World in order to practice their religion freely. English kings had authority to determine what religion their subjects would practice. Those who didn't follow the king's religion could be punished harshly. Puritans and Quakers were two groups from England that settled the new colonies seeking freedom of religion.

In September 1620, 102 English men, women, and children sailed to the New World on the

EXPLORE ONLINE

This chapter identifies various groups of people searching for a better life. The voyage to the New World was very difficult. To learn more about the ships the colonists traveled on, visit the website below. What new details did you learn?

The Mayflower Deconstructed
www.mycorelibrary.com/colonial-america

African slaves were kidnapped or sold into slavery by fellow Africans and then shipped to the New World.

Mayflower for 66 days. They had separated from the Church of England to practice their own religion. We know them as Pilgrims.

Servitude and Slavery

Those who wanted to come to the New World but couldn't afford the trip often came as indentured servants. They worked for their passage, food, and clothing. In the colonies they often helped clear land, farm, or build homes. After they had paid back what they owed through their work, they were able to work for money.

Not everyone who came to the New World came by choice. Some criminals were sent to the new settlements overseas. Other people were brought by force as slaves. Most of these people were taken from their homes in Africa and placed on ships. In the brutal system of slavery, African slaves were considered the property of those who purchased them. They were forced to work on farms or plantations. Some worked in the homes and businesses of white slave owners. Many masters treated their slaves harshly. Slaves were often beaten. Many were separated from their families when they were sold.

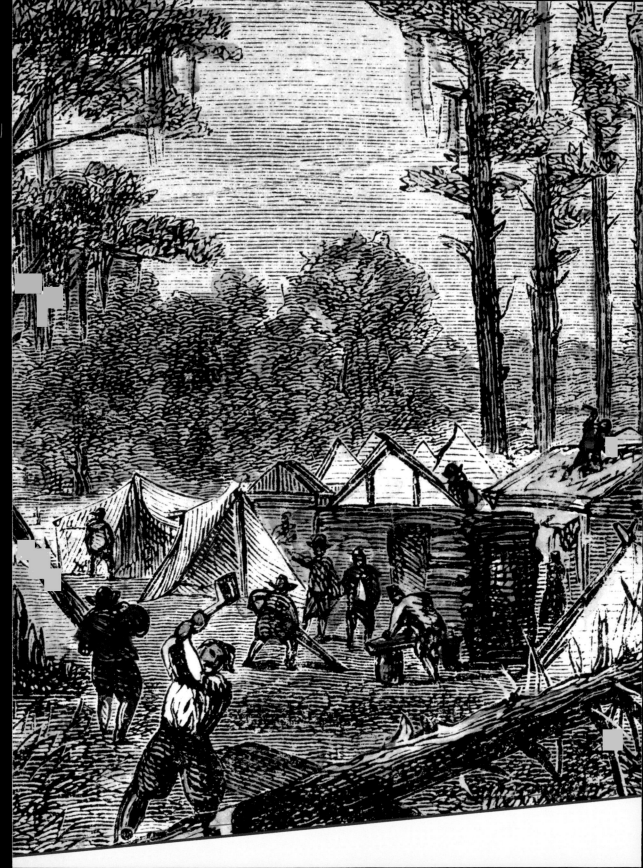

CHAPTER TWO

HARDSHIP AND SURVIVAL

Englilsh colonists landed in Virginia in the early 1600s. They settled Jamestown in 1605. Determined to get rich quick, many men went in search of gold instead of planting crops and preparing shelters for the cold winter. This was a deadly mistake. The supply of beef and pork brought from England didn't last long. Supply ships did not come as expected. The Jamestown settlers fished and ate

Settlers at a new colony such as Jamestown had hard work to do to ensure there was enough shelter and food to sustain the new colony.

The First Inhabitants

The Pueblos, Algonquians, and Iroquois were some of the first native peoples to interact with the Europeans. Some Native Americans helped the colonists grow food to survive. But Native Americans and colonists often had conflicting attitudes about owning land. Many Native Americans believed in communal ownership of resources. Colonists believed in individual ownership of pieces of land. These different ideas led to conflict between natives and newcomers.

anything they could hunt, including turtles, birds, and raccoons. When that failed, the desperate men also ate dogs, horses, and rats. By the fall of 1607, more than half the settlers had died.

Like the English colonists in Jamestown, those in the northern colonies struggled to find food, especially because they arrived in winter. England was slow to send supply ships. Everything had to be grown or caught. Starvation and sickness caused many deaths.

Settlers in the New England colonies used lumber from the abundant forests to build permanent homes.

Seeking Shelter

The first settlers built their shelters inside a palisade, or a wooden fence built for defense, to protect their small colony. Temporary homes were built out of sticks and brush. Settlers wove sticks together to make one room with a dirt floor. They used mud to fill in any holes.

Eventually colonists cleared land to make way for permanent homes. The abundant trees of New England were a great resource. Colonists built sawmills that could turn logs into usable planks of lumber.

Native American Dwellings

Many Native Americans in the northeast lived in dwellings called wigwams, wickiups, or wetus. Men built dome-shaped wooden frames, while women were in charge of covering the frames with bark or woven rushes. Wigwams were 15 to 20 feet (4.6–6.1 m) in diameter and 8 to 10 feet (2.4–3 m) tall. Wigwams were relatively easy to build and maintain.

Colonists dug cellars and drove heavy logs into the ground for support. Planks placed in an overlapping pattern made strong walls. Roofs were made with sod and bark. Colonists added lofts for sleeping and eventually staircases to replace crude ladders. Windows made of oiled paper allowed light in. Doorways were small and low, so people had to duck to enter through them. Small doors and windows kept large animals out.

Clay was common along the Atlantic coast, particularly in Virginia. Colonists shaped it into bricks, dried the bricks, and baked them in an oven. Homes made of brick were less likely to catch fire than those

Wigwam means "dwelling" in the Abenaki language, part of the Algonquian family of languages.

made of wood. The clay kept homes warm in the harsh winter months.

New England colonies grouped homes close together. Churches, taverns, and meeting halls created towns surrounded by farmland and pastures.

Many farmhouses were built in the Middle Colonies, which included New York, Pennsylvania, New Jersey, and Delaware. In order to acquire large areas of land, settlers often simply took land from the Native Americans who were already living there. The Native Americans usually resisted losing their land, which led to battles.

CHAPTER THREE

TRADE, COOPERATION, AND WAR

Native Americans and colonists had complex relationships that included periods of peace and periods of tension. The leader of the Jamestown settlement, Captain John Smith, befriended Chief Powhatan, leader of the Powhatan people who were living in the area. The two groups began trading. Early settlers were largely dependent on the native people for food. They traded for corn, turkey, pumpkins,

Native Americans traded with settlers all over North America.

Matoaka

In about 1607, John Smith met Matoaka, better known as Pocahontas. The daughter of Chief Powhatan, Matoaka often interacted with John Smith and the Jamestown colonists. She brought them much-needed gifts of food. When Matoaka was 17, the colonists took her prisoner. The colonists claimed the Powhatan had stolen weapons and attacked settlers. The colonists wanted English prisoners released and the weapons returned. Negotiations failed and Matoaka was never returned to her people. Eventually Matoaka married colonist John Rolfe. She and Rolfe traveled to Europe to promote the English colony. Matoaka grew ill and died soon after.

and fruit. Colonists also traded metal tools for furs and leather. The Native Americans introduced colonists to tobacco and other crops.

The colonists promised to trade guns and cannons to the Native Americans. But Smith did not want to arm the Native Americans with those weapons. When the Powhatan realized they would not be getting the weapons, they withdrew their corn, which angered the colonists. Bloody fights broke out often between the groups.

Samoset helped establish fruitful trade between Native Americans and settlers.

Many Native Americans were forced to leave their lands because of colonists' use of their superior firepower.

Other relationships between Native Americans and colonists were more friendly. In March 1621 an Algonquian named Samoset walked into Plymouth Colony and began talking to colonists in English. Samoset brought Squanto, a Patuxet man who had

Squanto

Squanto, also known as Tisquantum, was born in the early 1580s near Plymouth, Massachusetts. He was kidnapped by an English explorer and taken to England. In captivity he learned English. He returned to North America but was captured again and sold into slavery in Spain. Squanto managed to escape again and returned to his home in 1619. His entire Patuxet tribe had died from a smallpox epidemic. He went to live with the Wampanoag people. In 1621, Samoset introduced Squanto to the Pilgrims. Squanto became a member of the Plymouth colony and served as a guide and interpreter for the colonists.

been living with the Wampanoag people, to teach the Pilgrims how to plant corn, rye, and oats successfully. Squanto explained that placing fish in the ground with seeds helped fertilize the soil. In return for his help, the colonists offered the Wampanoag seeds they had brought with them from England.

New England colonists and Native Americans feasted on fruits including apples, pears, and cherries. Rabbit, venison, and squirrel were abundant

The Pilgrims of Plymouth Colony shared a harvest feast with the Wampanoag Native Americans in 1621.

and easily caught. With the Atlantic Ocean nearby, fish and eel were plentiful. All of these foods could be dried and stored for the harsh winter months.

The Wampanoag and Pilgrims feasted together in the fall of 1621 to celebrate a bountiful harvest and successful hunt. The Pilgrims and Native Americans ate outside. The men raced and fired guns. They communicated with each other as much as they could in their different languages. This was later called the first Thanksgiving. It was a peaceful time between the two groups, but the peace did not last.

The successful settlements in Virginia and New England encouraged other Europeans to cross the Atlantic. Some colonists already living in North America moved to other parts of the continent to create their own new settlements. Wherever they went, they brought conflicts over land ownership and diseases that wiped out native populations.

FURTHER EVIDENCE

Earlier in this book, the mystery of what happened to the settlers at Roanoke was discussed. What evidence was found? Go to the article about Roanoke at the website below. Historians are learning what happened to the settlers using science. What new evidence do they have? How does it help solve the mystery of Roanoke?

The Lost Colony of Roanoke
www.mycorelibrary.com/colonial-america

Colonists often wrote about their experiences with the native inhabitants. In this journal kept by Master George Percy, he describes his first sighting of Native Americans at Jamestown Colony:

> At night, when we were going aboard, there came the Savages creeping upon all fours, from the Hills, like Bears, with their Bows in their mouths, [who] charged us very desperately in the faces, hurt Captain Gabriel Archer in both his hands, and a sailor in two places of the body very dangerous. After they had spent their Arrows, and felt the sharpness of our shot, they retired into the Woods with a great noise, and so left us.

Source: "Jamestown: 1607, the First Months." Observations Gathered out of a Discourse of the Plantation of the Southern Colony in Virginia by the English, 1606. London: 1608. Web. Accessed July 29, 2014.

Changing Minds

This passage describes an English colonist's first experience with Native Americans. Why might a colonist use a word like "savage" to describe these people defending their homes? Think about what a Native American might have to say about encountering the Europeans for the first time. Write about the events described above from the point of view of one of the Native Americans. How might the Native Americans have felt about encountering strangers with dangerous weapons?

CHAPTER FOUR

WORK AND EDUCATION

The first colonists had put all their energy into simply surviving. But now that they had more secure food and shelter, colonists took up other jobs. Some jobs were needed in every colony. A miller was necessary to make flour for bread. Blacksmiths smelted iron to create farming tools and weapons. Artisans made furniture, containers, fences, and silverware. Women also had important jobs, including

Mills were often powered by wind or water.

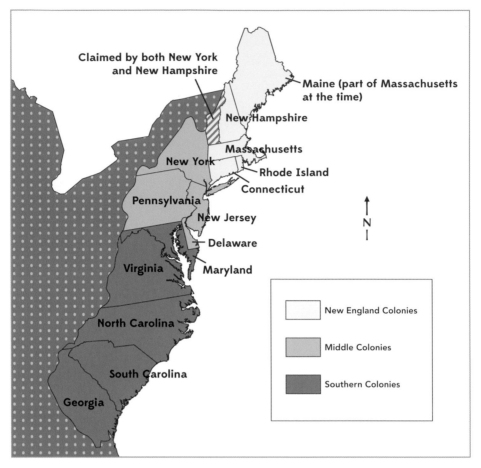

Map of the 13 Colonies

There were 13 original colonies. According to the chapter, what jobs were common in the different colonies? Why might those jobs have been common in those places?

raising children and overseeing their education. Women also grew, gathered, and preserved most of the food. They spun, wove, and sewed clothing.

Shipbuilding provided work for many colonists.

Different Lands, Different Jobs

Other jobs varied by colony. Shipbuilding and whaling were important in the New England colonies. Carpenters built ships. Sail makers, rope makers, and blacksmiths outfitted them. Sailors made up their crew. Whaling provided ivory, blubber, and oil for light. Many indentured servants and slaves worked in the whaling industry.

In the Middle Colonies corn and wheat grew well. Rivers provided power for mills to grind grain. The land was rich with iron, creating jobs for miners.

Tobacco

Colonist leader John Rolfe recognized the importance of growing tobacco. By 1630, Jamestown was exporting more than 1 million pounds of tobacco to countries in Europe every year. Indentured servants and slaves were used in the tobacco fields, providing cheap or free forced labor. Since they did not have to pay their workers much, tobacco planters made more money. Tobacco farmers grew rich and many in the colonies prospered.

Farming continued to be an important occupation throughout the colonies. But instead of growing food only to feed their families, farmers grew crops to sell to other colonies and countries.

The Southern Colonies were known for their plantations. Plantations were large farms that used slave labor to produce crops to sell. Tobacco was a crop that made some colonists especially rich. The wealthiest colonists owned plantations spanning thousands of acres. Warehouses, slave quarters, and chapels were built alongside the mansions. As in the Middle Colonies, settlers in the

Plantation slaves often lived on the grounds of the plantations where they were forced to work.

South often forced Native Americans off the land to build their plantations.

Education in the Colonies

All children who were not slaves received some form of instruction. The style of education differed by region and background. Many colonists, such as the Puritans, thought it was important to be able to read the Bible. *The New England Primer* was published in 1690 in Massachusetts and was used to teach reading to some children. Some women taught local children while tending to chores in their homes. These schools were called dame schools. At age eight, boys could continue on to grammar school to learn writing, reading, and arithmetic. Girls might learn writing in the home, but usually learned only household duties.

Education in the Middle Colonies was mostly left to families until the 1680s, when a Pennsylvania law required that all children be taught to read and write. Pennsylvania's first school soon opened.

In the Southern Colonies, education primarily took place at home. Plantations were large and most children did not live as close together as in other colonies. Wealthy families hired tutors. As boys grew

PERSPECTIVES
Slaves

Most slaves worked in the fields, doing hard, repetitive work regardless of weather. Other slaves were house servants. Some slaves learned a trade and worked as blacksmiths or carpenters. Slaves in the New England colonies often worked aboard ships in the whaling industry. Most slaves were not allowed to receive an education.

Many children learned to read and write in order to study the Bible.

older, they might be sent to England to finish their schooling. Girls learned reading, writing, and basic arithmetic skills so they could run the home.

Taking Up a Trade

After boys received a basic education, most got a job or possibly had an apprenticeship. This meant they learned a skill or trade from someone with experience. Boys often learned their father's craft. While it was

Girls learned to sew at a young age.

not common for girls to have an apprenticeship, some trained to be dressmakers. More often, girls practiced skills such as sewing and knitting that would be useful in running a household and raising children.

The *New England Primer* was the most popular textbook in Colonial America. The *Primer* taught children to read and about various topics. Each letter and phrase accompanied a matching picture:

A - *In Adam's Fall, We sinned all.*

B - *Thy life to mend, This Book attend.*

C - *The Cat doth play, and after slay.*

D - *A Dog will bite A thief at night.*

E - *An Eagle's flight Is out of sight*

Source: The New England Primer. *Benjamin Harris, 1688. Print.*

Consider Your Audience

Review this passage closely. How does this schoolbook compare with yours? Write some phrases of your own that modern students could use to study letters. How does your lesson differ from the one in the *New England Primer*?

CHAPTER FIVE

COLONIES NO MORE

Great Britain ruled the 13 colonies along the eastern coast of North America by 1763. They gained new colonies through conquest and trade with other colonial powers such as Spain and the Netherlands. The colonies stretched from present-day Maine to Georgia. Great Britain also had colonies in the Caribbean. By 1775 the colonists were more than 2 million strong. They had thrived while Native

European diseases took a heavy toll on Native American populations.

Native Americans in the Southeast

Native Americans in the Southeast were mostly farmers who lived in small villages and large towns. The Spanish explorer Hernando de Soto came to present-day Florida in 1539. At first the Native Americans welcomed de Soto. But he forced many Native Americans into slavery. The Native Americans fought back, but their numbers were quickly reduced by warfare and disease. The Spanish sold many of the surviving Native Americans into slavery and converted others to Christianity.

Americans had been killed off by war and disease.

Impacts on Native American Populations

Of the approximately 12 million Native Americans who inhabited North America in 1500, only 600,000 remained by 1800. That means more than 90 percent of the native population died due to epidemic diseases such as smallpox, and because of warfare with the European settlers. Diseases such as measles, influenza, cholera, and scarlet fever wiped out entire groups. Native populations had no defense against the entirely

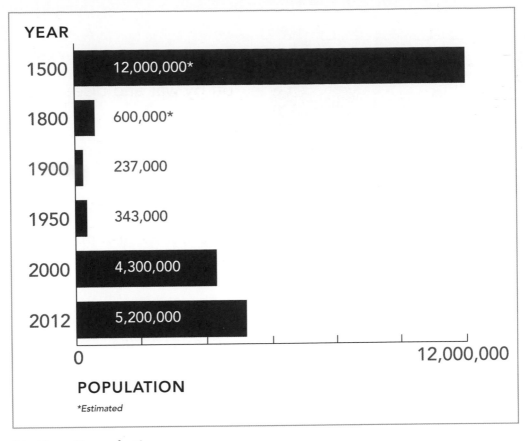

YEAR

1500	12,000,000*
1800	600,000*
1900	237,000
1950	343,000
2000	4,300,000
2012	5,200,000

0   12,000,000

POPULATION

Estimated

Native Populations

The graph above shows how Native American populations changed over time. How does seeing the graph help you understand the information concerning Native American population declines that you read about in the book? Why might Native American populations have begun to recover after 1900?

unfamiliar European diseases. Many Native American children starved to death when many adults were too stricken by illness to provide food. During and after the colonial period, Native Americans were

Great Britain's redcoat soldiers won many battles against the French in North America.

forced off their ancestral lands into smaller and smaller reservations while European settlers and their descendants expanded across the continent.

The Road to Revolution

The British government paid to protect its colonies. Great Britain supplied the weapons and soldiers used to fight wars in the colonies. They helped the colonists fight against Native Americans and against other European powers such as the French. These conflicts were very expensive. The British government raised taxes on the colonists to pay for the soldiers. This angered some colonists. They felt the taxes were unfair. They wanted local leaders to decide their taxes. Leaders from the colonies met to decide what to do. At first, most colonists only wanted the right to govern themselves as part of the British Empire. But Great Britain would not give in to colonists' demands. Some colonists began dreaming of independence. The colonial way of life was about to change forever. The Revolutionary War was about to begin.

Medicine in Colonial Times

In colonial times, people did not fully understand germs and disease. They believed the body contained different humors, or fluids. When a person had an illness, it was believed these humors were unbalanced. A common cure for many illnesses was bleeding, or letting out large amounts of a person's blood. People thought that this would remove whatever was making the patient ill. Leeches were sometimes placed on a patient to suck out the blood in a process called leeching.

Sara is a ten-year-old girl on a Pennsylvania farm in the 1700s. She shares a room with her many brothers and sisters.

5:00 a.m.

Sara grabs the buckets and walks down to the creek to get fresh water. She collects twigs and sticks for the fire. Her sister gathers berries. Sara checks for eggs. Finding none, she helps her sister make the butter. She gets blisters on her hands from working the churn.

8:00 a.m.

Sara begins weaving. Today she will learn to make a new shirt for her father. Her mother is feeding the baby. When she is finished she will help Sara read.

9:00 a.m.

The children begin lessons for the day. Sara practices writing. Mother gets the Bible. She only lets the eldest children hold it. They take turns reading. Sara knows the most words.

1:00 p.m.

After dinner Sara goes to work on the farm. She collects carrots and lettuce as well as rosemary and thyme. The family will use the ingredients for supper.

3:00 p.m.

The children come outside to complete their chores. Some of Sara's brothers butcher one of the pigs. Others go to work in the fields. Sara must finish the weaving.

6:00 p.m.

The children set the table for the evening meal. Afterward, as the grownups talk, the girls clean up the meal and head to bed. Tomorrow the family starts planning for the coming winter months.

STOP AND THINK

Why Do I Care?

The first colonists came to the United States more than 400 years ago. Reflect on what you have read in this book and consider what has changed in this country since that time. Compare the colonists' homes, food, and schooling to yours. What is the same? What is different?

You Are There

This book discusses the voyage colonists took across the Atlantic. When colonists first arrived in the New World, there were no buildings, farms, or roads. Imagine you have just arrived in what will become the Jamestown Colony. You have no idea what animals are living in the woods or what you will eat. How do you feel? What will you do first?

Say What?

Learning about different cultures and time periods can introduce readers to new words. Find five words you did not understand before reading this book. Use the glossary or a dictionary to help you figure out what the words mean. Then use each word in a sentence.

Take a Stand

You read that colonists and native groups often battled over land. What did they disagree about? Who do you think had the more convincing argument? Write a persuasive essay as if you are a colonist or a Native American. Be sure to give reasons for your opinion.

GLOSSARY

artisan
a worker in a skilled trade, especially one that involves making things by hand

colonies
settlements ruled by another country

epidemic
widespread occurrence of an infectious disease in a community at a particular time

indentured servant
a person who is placed under contract to work for another person over a period of time, usually in return for travel expenses or shelter

palisade
a fence, usually made of wood, forming an enclosure for defense purposes

pilgrim
a person who travels for religious reasons

provisions
a supply of food, drink, and/or equipment, especially for a journey

slave
a person who is the legal property of another and forced to obey them

LEARN MORE

Books

Hamen, Susan. *The Thirteen Colonies*. Edina, MN: Abdo, 2013.

McGovern, Ann. *If You Lived in Colonial Times*. New York: Scholastic Press, 1992.

Youcha, Geraldine. *Minding the Children: Child Care in America from Colonial Times to Present*. Boston: Da Capo Press, 2009.

Websites

To learn more about Daily Life in US History, visit **booklinks.abdopublishing.com.** These links are routinely monitored and updated to provide the most current information available.

Visit **www.mycorelibrary.com** for free additional tools for teachers and students.

INDEX

ABOUT THE AUTHOR

Julia Garstecki is a teacher and writer who lives with her family in Chautauqua, New York. She loves researching topics and writing about them. Julia encourages her students to do the same!